ICT

Invites,
Posters and
Presentations

Anne Rooney

QED Publishing

First published in the UK in 2004 by
QED Publishing
A Quarto Group Company
226 City Road
London, EC1V 2TT

www.qed-publishing.co.uk

A Catalogue record for this book is available
from the British Library.

ISBN 1 84538 276 5

Written by Anne Rooney
Consultant Philip Stubbs
Designed by Jacqueline Palmer
Editor Anna Claybourne
Illustrator John Haslam
Photographer Ray Moller
Models supplied by Scallywags
Additional artwork by Luki Sumner-Rooney

Creative Director Louise Morley
Editorial Manager Jean Coppendale

Printed and bound in China

The words in **bold** are
explained in the Glossary
on page 31.

Contents

What's it all about?

We all communicate in lots of different ways. We chat on the phone, read, watch TV and videos, send emails and texts, and look at web pages. This book is all about communicating with written words.

Written communication is not just about writing, though. Take a look at a few magazines and newspapers and you'll see that they have pictures, tables, lists, headings, captions, graphs – all kinds of extras to help to get the message across.

In this book, you'll learn to do the same – make your words lively and exciting, and arrange them so that they're easy to understand.

On paper or on screen?

You can write with a pencil or pen on a piece of paper – or you can write using a computer.

Visit The Zoo

We're going to concentrate on writing on the computer using a word processor. But don't forget alternatives to the computer – sometimes paper and pens are still the best way!

Think before you speak – and before you write! You can save yourself a lot of work if you know what you're trying to do before you start.

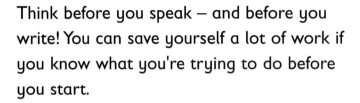

Who, what, why?

Here are some things to ask yourself before you begin:

- What do I want to say?
- Who do I want to say it to?
- Why am I saying it at all?

What you want to say will be the **content** of your work. The people you want to say it to are your **audience**. Why you are saying it is your **purpose**.

What will the content be?

Work out what you want to say before you start, so you can make sure you've included everything you need. Only say things that are relevant and don't wander off on a different topic.

Who's the audience?

You need to match your words and the way they're arranged (the **layout**) to what your audience expects and can read. If you say it in the wrong way, people might not understand or take notice. For example, you wouldn't use the same words in a report for your teacher as in an email to your seven-year-old cousin.

Why am I saying it?

The purpose of your writing will help you to decide what type of document to make and what extras to put in it. You might want to use a picture, a table or a chart to help get your message across. If you want to give people directions, for example, you could add a map.

Let's add a map to make it really clear!

We can post a printout to Auntie Abigail, and email it to everyone else!

How to find our house

Our house is at the end of Long Lane, off the High Street. Don't look for a house number – it doesn't have one!

High Street

Long Lane

Getting started

Should you be using the computer at all? For a birthday card, it might be easier just to draw it on a piece of paper. If it's important that the writing is really neat, or if it's a long document you might want to change later, a computer is best.

Here are some things to think about:

- If you create your work on the computer, you can change it easily.

- If you create your work on paper, you can add extra bits, like stickers and glitter, cut holes, add flaps ...

- It's easy to create a really impressive-looking document on the computer – and the words and letters will be perfectly neat.

- If you create a document on the computer, you can re-use all or part of it later in another document.

Remember that you can start your work on the computer and add extras, like drawings, after you've printed it out.

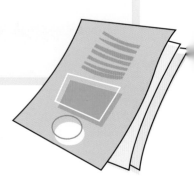

Make a plan

It's a good idea to plan the main points you want to make before you start writing, especially if you're doing a complicated piece of work. Then collect your ideas, notes and any source materials you need, and you're ready to go.

My tigers project
• What are tigers?
• Where they live
• What they eat
• Tiger cubs
• Saving the tiger

Starting to write

Once you've worked out what you want to say, you need to type it into the computer.

Space bar

Remember to use:

- The space bar (once only) to add a space between words.

Shift key

- The Shift key to get a capital letter.

- The Backspace key to get rid of a letter if you've typed the wrong one.

Backspace key

- The Enter or Return key to start a new line – but only when you get to the end of a paragraph, or a line in a list. The rest of the time, just keep typing: the computer will automatically start a new line for you when you need one.

Return key

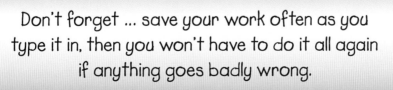

Don't forget ... save your work often as you type it in, then you won't have to do it all again if anything goes badly wrong.

Making sense

All documents need to communicate a message, whether it's 'come to my party' or the details of your investigation of minibeasts. This means your document must make sense!

The right words for the right people

You should always write as clearly as you can, but sometimes you need to be extra careful to make things simple. Imagine there's been a flood in the school toilets, and you've been asked to make some posters warning people that the floor is wet.

If you were writing only for adults, you might put:

For little children, you would use simpler words that they would understand:

A picture would make it even better, especially for smaller children:

Beware! Danger of flooding

Look out! Wet floor!

Look out! Wet floor!

Putting things in order

Begin by working out the order you want to put your main points in. You should start with an introduction, then have a paragraph or section for each point, and finish by summing up what you've said.

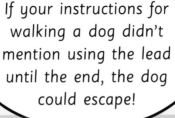

Sometimes, the order is particularly important. If you're writing a set of instructions, you have to put the steps in the right order or else they won't work.

If your instructions for walking a dog didn't mention using the lead until the end, the dog could escape!

List of some things to do on our holiday

1 Go horse riding
2 Go swimming
3 Visit Castle
4 Cake shop

What matters most?

You may need to put items in order of importance, especially if you think some people might not read right to the end.

In a long piece of writing, you need to work out a good structure, so that people can find important ideas easily, and don't lose the thread of what they're reading.

If you're making a list, put the most important things first.

11

Organizing information

To make your documents easier to read, it helps to break down what you're saying into short chunks. It doesn't all have to be arranged in paragraphs either. Some information is easier to understand as a list or a table.

Headings and sections

To help people see where a long essay is going, you might divide it into sections with headings.

Each article in a newspaper or magazine has a heading so you can see what it's about. You'll need to do this if you're making a newsletter.

Don't forget a title for the whole document too, so that people know what they're about to read.

The solar system

The Sun

The Sun is just one of the trillions of stars in the Universe. It is in the middle of the solar system, and the planets revolve around it.

Mars

Mars is the fourth planet away from the Sun. It is smaller than the Earth and its gravity is not as strong. Mars looks red because of all the iron in its rocks.

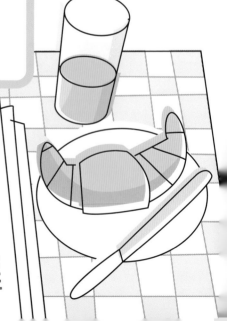

The Jedley News

Bear bites man at Jedley zoo

Hole in cage!

Family day out

Big teeth

New statue in park

Lists

Sometimes a list is the best way to present information. To show a sequence of things, or the order of importance of several items, use a numbered list. If the order doesn't matter, you can use a list with bullets.

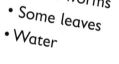

DO IT!

Look for a button for making a list with numbers or bullets. Select your text (see page 14), then click on the button. Or you can click the button first, then start typing your list.

Planning an experiment

1. Work out your aim
2. Choose your equipment
3. Carry out the experiment
4. Work out your conclusion

Equipment

You will need:

- A tub of earth
- Three worms
- Some leaves
- Water

Make a table

A table lines up text in columns and rows. It lets you show lots of facts or figures in a small space.

DO IT!

Look for an option to 'Insert Table', 'Add Table' or 'Draw Table'. Alternatively, you can use the Tab key to line up your text or numbers in columns.

How people in class 4X travel to school:

	Bike	Car	Walk	Bus	Total
Girls	7	5	4	1	17
Boys	6	7	3	0	16
Total	13	12	7	1	33

Looking good

The way your text looks should suit the **audience** and **purpose** of the document. Really wacky lettering and lots of colours might be great for a party invitation or poster, but they're not so good in a report on a science project.

Think about:

- The style, colour and size of the letters you're using.

- Using pictures to illustrate your text.

- Putting in headings and other special kinds of text.

- The way the pictures and words are arranged on the page.

Selecting text

You'll need to select text in order to change the way it looks.

1. Put the **cursor** at the start of the text you want to select.

2. Press and hold down the mouse button and move the mouse so that the text is highlighted.

3. Lift your finger off the mouse button when all the text you want is highlighted.

You can usually select all the text in your document at once, too. Look for a menu option called 'Select All'.

One part of this text has been selected. It is the type that is white on black instead of black on white.

Trial and error

Don't be afraid to experiment! It's easy to change things on a computer. Save different versions of your work with different names, so you can compare your designs and pick the best one.

Fun with fonts

The **font** is the style and shape of the letters. There might be lots of different fonts on your computer – take a look.

Fonts can be Fun
Fonts can be Fun
FONTS CAN BE FUN
Fonts can be Fun

Pick the right font

Some fonts are easier to read than others. Fancy or dramatic fonts are good for making small bits of text stand out. Simple, clean-looking fonts are better for long blocks of text, as they're easier to read.

Picture fonts

Your computer might have some fonts that show little pictures. These are symbol fonts. You can use them to add symbols or pictures to your work. Because they are text, you can make them bigger or smaller by changing the text size.

Good for posters

Good for long essays

Text effects, styles & sizes

You can use special effects and different font styles and sizes to help get your message across.

Text effects

Try out different effects and styles to make your text more exciting.

These words are bold

These words are italic

These are <u>underlined</u>

These are outlined

These are shadowed

Changing colour

You can change the colour of your text. Just select the text, and click on a colour from the colour menu.

Remember that your colours will only show up on a printout if you're using a colour printer. Otherwise, they'll come out grey.

class of
2004

MARIA
Class joker
"You've got something on your face – oh, it's your nose."

RAJ
Future NASA scientist
"3... 2... 1... Liftoff!"

MAX
Head in the clouds
"Is it 2004 already?"

ANNA
Teacher's fave
"I can't believe we're leaving!"

DO IT!

Select the text you want to change. Look for a menu option such as 'Font', 'Text style' or 'Text effects', and buttons that show the style of text you want, like this:

B *I* <u>U</u> O S

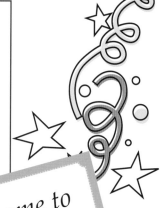

Text size

Text size is usually shown in **point size**. This is a special measurement that comes from old-style printing. There are 72 points in an inch (2.5cm). The text in this book is 14 point – a good size for the main text of a long piece of writing.

SCHOOL REPORT

This is my report on 10-point text. 10-point text is quite small, so it's perfect if you want to fit in lots of words.

To make it easy to read, it helps to break your text up into short paragraphs.

Please come to my 20-point text party

DO IT!

Select the text you want to change. Look for a box where you can type in the text size you want, or a menu offering different sizes you can choose.

BEWARE

36 POINT TEXT

Say what you mean

Try using different colours, sizes and styles to add to or emphasize the meaning of your words.

splash   computer

prickle   *fancy*

Dracula   thin

spooky   gro**w**th   sport

Pictures

Most documents look better with pictures, or diagrams to help explain things. Sometimes, the picture can be the most important part of all.

Where do I get pictures?

You can get pictures onto the computer in lots of ways.

- If you have a **digital camera**, you can take a digital photo and load it into the computer.

- If you have a **scanner**, you can scan in pictures you've drawn on paper.

- You can use an **art program** on the computer to paint or draw a picture.

- You can use **clip art** – ready-made pictures that you can get on CD-ROM or from the World Wide Web.

The solar system

The Sun

The Sun is just one of the trillions of stars in the Universe. It is in the middle of the solar system, and the planets revolve around it.

Mars

Mars is the fourth planet away from the Sun. It is smaller than the Earth and its gravity is not as strong. Mars looks red because

Placing a picture

Think carefully about where on the page you want your picture to be, and how big it should be. Keep pictures near the text they go with.

Sometimes, the picture is the biggest thing on the page.

LOST!

Have you seen Alice?

DO IT!

Look for an option like 'Insert picture', 'Insert clip art' or 'Add picture'.

There might be some drawing tools in your text program that let you draw a simple picture straight onto the page.

If you save a picture you've made on the computer, make sure it's a type of file your word processor can read. You might need to ask for help with this.

Do it by hand

Don't forget you can draw extra things on the page after you've printed your work out. So if you don't have a scanner or art program, you can just leave a space on the page and fill it in later.

Picture sizes

If you need to make a picture bigger or smaller when it's in your document, look for little blocks, called 'handles', at the corners of the picture, and click on and drag these to change the size.

You can also move a picture around by clicking on the middle of it and dragging it.

If you drag a handle on a side, rather than a corner, your picture might become squashed or stretched.

Arranging text

The way text is arranged, lined up and spaced affects how good it looks and how easy it is to read.

Text alignment

Alignment means the way the text lines up between the edges of the page. Most of the text in this book is left-aligned.

Titles are often **centred**, which means they are lined up in the middle of the page.

This line is centred

Picture captions are sometimes right-aligned. They line up at the ends of the lines, on the right-hand side of the page.

This line is right-aligned

Keep it clear

Centred text and right-aligned text are good for special effects but they're quite hard to read, so don't over-use them.

DO IT!

Look for buttons with pictures of text alignments, like these:

Or look for options like 'Align Text', 'Right Align' or 'Center Text'.

Solar System News

Moon landing planned
Astronauts are planning to set foot on the Moon again. It will be the first trip to the Moon for over 30 years.

The Moon

Solar flares
Scientists have reported that solar flares have been extra-large and extra-strong in recent months. They can affect computers and make them stop working.

Different styles for different sections

If you look at a magazine or book, you'll see that lots of different styles of text are used for different types of text. You can use different styles of text in your own work too. Try to match the way the text looks with how important that part is.

Minibeasts

Minibeasts get their name because they're smaller than most other animals. They include insects, spiders, worms, slugs and snails.

Minibeasts without legs

Many minibeasts have no legs at all. They simply slide, slither or burrow their way around.

A giant African land snail

Snails
A snail moves along the ground by rippling the underside of its body. It also releases a slippery slime to help it move.

Worms
Worms' bodies are made up of segments.

Headings and subheadings

Your main heading should be bigger than the subheadings that split the text up. Make headings look striking by changing the **font**, text size and colour. Don't forget you can use underlining, bold or other styles if you like.

Main text and other text

Pick a font, size and style for your main text, then choose other styles for other types of text. For example, you could use a big, bold style for the introduction to help your readers get started.

Staying the same

When you use different styles, make sure you use them consistently. This means always using the same font and style for text of the same sort — captions, for example.

Watch out!
Don't use too many different fonts and colours, as your work will start to look messy and it will distract people from what your document says.

Page layout

The way your document is arranged on the page is called the **layout**. By putting text in columns or adding space, you can make a document look better.

Margins and columns

Most documents have areas of white space around the edges of the page, called margins. Big margins give the page a more spacious look and make it easier for people to read.

Putting text in two or more columns is effective if you're making a newsletter.

DO IT!

Look for a button or menu option called 'Columns' or 'Number of columns'.

Pictures and text

Think about where to put the pictures. They'll look better if they're spread out evenly through the text. If they're rectangular, line them up carefully so that they don't look too untidy.

Football club

Would you like to come to a football club after school?

Meet in the gym on Thursday at 3pm

Find out more from Darrell (year 6)

Football club

Would you like to come to a football club after school?

Meet in the gym on Thursday at 3pm

Find out more from Darrell (year 6)

Solar System News

Moon landing

Astronauts are planning to set foot on the Moon again. It will be the first trip to the Moon for over 30 years. Experts say it won't have changed much.

The Moon

Solar flares

Scientists have reported that solar flares have been extra-large and extra-

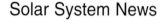

Blank space

Empty space on the page is very helpful for your readers. It's hard to read words that are very cramped and crowded together. Leave space between paragraphs and around pictures, and make sure the margins are large enough.

Jedley Primary School Drama Club presents
Jack and the Beanstalk

Directed by	Katie Edwards	Scene 1	In the village
Music by	Nick Grainger	Scene 2	Jack's house
Jack	Luke McAllister	Scene 3	In the forest
Jack's Mum	Ryan Anderson		Interval
Old woman	Amelia Harper	Scene 4	Jack's house
King Beany	Shahid Yousef	Scene 5	Giant's castle
Princess Poppy	Tora Jones	Scene 6	King's palace
Giant's voice	Anthony Kim		
Daisy the cow	Jake Murdoch and Paul Paterson		

The Interval will be 20 minutes long. Refreshments will be served in room 4X.

The Drama Club would like to thank Stitches fabric shop, Jedley for their donation of the materials used to make the beanstalk.

Jedley Primary School Drama Club
presents
Jack and the Beanstalk

Directed by Katie Edwards
Music by Nick Grainger

Jack	Luke McAllister	Scene 1	In the village
Jack's Mum	Ryan Anderson	Scene 2	Jack's house
Old woman	Amelia Harper	Scene 3	In the forest
King Beany	Shahid Yousef		Interval
Princess Poppy	Tora Jones	Scene 4	Jack's house
Giant's Voice	Anthony Kim	Scene 5	Giant's castle
Daisy the cow	Jake Murdoch and Paul Paterson	Scene 6	King's palace

The Interval will be 20 minutes long.
Refreshments will be served in room 4X.

The Drama Club would like to thank Stitches fabric shop, Jedley for their donation of the materials used to make the beanstalk.

DO IT!

To set the space around the page, look for an option like 'Set margins', 'Page margins', 'Page setup' or 'Page layout'.

To add space between paragraphs or pictures, use the Enter or Return key to add a blank line.

Perfect!

So you've entered all the words and made them look good, but your work's not quite done yet. You need to **review** it and see if you can improve it.

Ask for help

It's not always easy to judge how good your own work is, so it's a good idea to get a friend, parent or other checker to look at it, too. You – and your checker – should ask:

- Does the document get across the message I wanted it to effectively?

- Are the words suited to the **audience** and purpose?

- Does it look right?

- How could I make my work even better?

Making changes

Maybe your work would be better if parts of it were moved around. To move a chunk of text, you'll need to:

1. Select the text you want to move.

2. Choose a 'Cut' button or menu option to cut the text.

3. Put the cursor to where you want to move the text.

4. Use a 'Paste' button or menu option to put the text back in.

Find and replace

If you want to change a word all the way through a document, you can use **find and replace**. For example, if you'd written a report on Julius Caesar, but typed his name in wrong, you could find all the times you had used 'Juluis' and change them to 'Julius'.

Find and Replace	
Find what:	Juluis
Replace with:	Julius

Replace | Replace all | Find next | Cancel

DO IT!

Look for a menu option such as 'Find and replace' or 'Search and replace'. Then just type in the words you want to find, and what you want to change them to.

Spellchecking

Your word processor may have a spellchecker. It checks the words you've used and compares them with its own dictionary. Look out – a spellchecker sometimes misses words that are spelled wrongly, or tells you a word is wrong even if it isn't, because it doesn't recognize it. If you use a spellchecker, check your work yourself too.

All finished

When you've improved and checked your work, you can print out your final copies. Save your work again before you print it, just in case anything goes wrong. Print just one copy first so that you can check it a final time, before you print any extra copies.

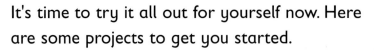

Projects to try

It's time to try it all out for yourself now. Here are some projects to get you started.

Use your eyes

Firstly, here's a project you can add to at any time. Why not start now? Collect all sorts of written documents. Include posters, leaflets, cards, labels, magazines, books, tickets... anything! Then take a good look at them.

Look at how words are used, the fonts that have been chosen, the shape and layout of the pictures, and the styles used for different kinds of text.

Looking at documents around you gives you a good 'eye' for design and sparks ideas of your own.

How much white space is there on the page? Is there anything unusual or surprising? Do you think the document does its job well? Could you improve it?

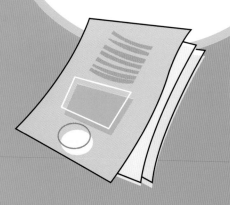

Make a poster

Design a poster to advertise a club, a play or a sports event you're in. How will you make people stop and look at the poster? How will you persuade them your event or club is really good?

WHAT ARE YOU
DOING ON FRIDAY?

COME TO OUR
SPORTS DAY

Top tips

• Don't use too many words. If it looks too long, people won't read it. Go for a really striking design.

• Try using a question, such as 'Where will you be on Saturday?'

• Use colour and pictures to make your poster stand out – especially if you're going to put it up near lots of other posters.

How to...

Try writing a set of instructions for a friend to follow. Pick something that's not too hard – how to make a paper plane or a folded fortune teller, for instance. Make sure you start with a list of things they'll need. Then put the stages in order. Add pictures if you think that will be useful.

Ask a friend to try following your instructions. Do they work? Could you improve them? Would changing the layout make them easier to follow?

T-shirt factory

Use a text program to make your own t-shirts with wacky slogans or messages.

You will need:

- Iron-on transfer paper for printing your design
- A plain t-shirt – white is best
- A printer

Here's what to do:

Beware – fierce boy

1. Think of a slogan to add to your t-shirt. It could be something funny, or maybe your favourite poem, or a verse from a song that you like.

Beware fierce boy

2. Type in your text and arrange it as you want it. Make the text big, so that people can read it without having to get too close! Remember it will need to fit on a sheet of transfer paper.

You can use colour (as long as you have a colour printer). Choose colours that are bright enough to show up.

3. Print your design on normal paper first and check the spelling and layout. Make any changes you think will improve it.

4. Finally, print your design onto a sheet of special t-shirt transfer paper. To make the writing show the right way round on the t-shirt, you'll probably have to print the slogan in reverse. Look for an option called 'Print in reverse', 'Back-to-front' or 'Mirror image'.

You could make a t-shirt as a great present for a friend.

5. Follow the instructions on the pack to iron the design onto your t-shirt. Ask an adult to help with this.

Working with Words

This book will help a child to:

- Prepare a report on a history or science topic as a word-processed document

- Re-order text in an English class

- Prepare a sequence of instructions on the computer

- Write up a project on the computer and illustrate it with scanned pictures, clip-art, or original pictures produced on the computer.

Working with Words helps children to practise essential skills and tools they will need throughout their education, putting them on the road to good working habits. These include: writing on paper or on screen; planning and organizing work; drafting a document; developing ideas into structured text; revising and improving text; checking spelling and grammar; presenting a clean copy; evaluating and discussing their work.

Work with your children to enable them to incorporate planning, drafting, checking, and reviewing their work in all projects they do and as a matter of habit. Ask them to discuss how their work could be improved, whether computer methods are the best choice for a job at hand, and how computer methods compare with manual methods.

National Curriculum resources online

ICT programme of study at Key Stage 2 in the National Curriculum:

www.nc.uk.net/nc/contents/ICT-2--POS.html

On teaching ICT in other subject areas:

www.ncaction.org.uk/subjects/ict/inother.htm

ICT schemes of work
(you can download a printable copy):

www.standards.dfes.gov.uk/schemes2/it/

The schemes of work for Key Stage 2 suggest ways that ICT can be taught in years 3–6.

Resources

The Internet is a rich source of fonts and clip-art, both of which are valuable resources for working with text.

Use a search engine to search for
fonts+free+download
or clipart+free+download

If you want a picture of something in particular, add this to your search
(for example, clipart+free+download+ Christmas tree)

It's a good idea to include the words "for children" when searching for clip-art. A good collection of clip-art suitable for children is at:

www.kidsdomain.com/clip/

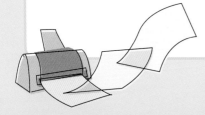

Glossary

Alignment

How text is lined up between the page margins. Left-aligned text starts at the left of the page. Right-aligned text lines up at the ends of the lines, on the right-hand side of the page.

Art program

Computer program for making drawings or paintings on screen.

Audience

The people who you hope will read your document.

Centred text

Text that's lined up in the middle of the page.

Clip art

Ready-made pictures to put in your documents or use in other pictures.

Content

The subject matter of your writing.

Cursor

Small vertical line or block on screen that shows where text you type will appear.

Digital camera

Camera that stores pictures in a memory chip rather than on a film.

Find and replace

Find one word or phrase, and replace it with another word or phrase.

Font

Style of letters. All the letters in a font have a similar appearance.

Layout

The arrangement of words and pictures on the page.

Point size

Measurement for text.

Purpose

The aim of your document.

Review

Look through and evaluate.

Scanner

Device for copying pictures from paper into the computer.

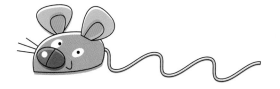

Index